DETAILS

Name:	
Company:	
Contact Number:	
Contact Number:	
Email:	

Emergency Details:

Name:	Name:
Company:	Company:

Important:

Date:		**Day:**	Mon	Tue	Wed	Thu	Fri	Sat	Sun

Foreman:

Contract No:

Hours Lost Due To Bad Weather

Visitors

Weather Conditions

AM	PM

Schedule

Completion Date:

Days Ahead of Schedute:

Days Behind Schedute:

Problems / Delays

Safely Issues:

Accidents/Incidents:

Summary Of Work Performed Today

Signature:

Name:

Equipment On Site	No Units	Working	
		Yes	No

Employee /Contractor	Trade	Contracted Hours	Overtime

Materials Delivered	From & Rate	Equipment Rented	No Units

Notes:

Date:		**Day:**	Mon	Tue	Wed	Thu	Fri	Sat	Sun

Foreman:

Contract No:

Hours Lost Due To Bad Weather

Visitors

Weather Conditions

AM	PM

Schedule

Completion Date:

Days Ahead of Schedute:

Days Behind Schedute:

Problems / Delays

Safely Issues:

Accidents/Incidents:

Summary Of Work Performed Today

Signature:

Name:

Equipment On Site	No Units	Working	
		Yes	No

Employee /Contractor	Trade	Contracted Hours	Overtime

Materials Delivered	From & Rate	Equipment Rented	No Units

Notes:

Date:		**Day:**	Mon Tue Wed Thu Fri Sat Sun
Foreman:			
Contract No:			

Hours Lost Due To Bad Weather

Visitors

Weather Conditions

AM	PM

Schedule

Completion Date:	
Days Ahead of Schedute:	
Days Behind Schedute:	

Problems / Delays

Safely Issues:

Accidents/Incidents:

Summary Of Work Performed Today

Signature:	Name:

Equipment On Site	No Units	Working	
		Yes	No

Employee /Contractor	Trade	Contracted Hours	Overtime

Materials Delivered	From & Rate	Equipment Rented	No Units

Notes:

Date:		Day:	Mon	Tue	Wed	Thu	Fri	Sat	Sun

Foreman:

Contract No:

Hours Lost Due To Bad Weather

Visitors

Weather Conditions

AM	PM

Schedule

Completion Date:

Days Ahead of Schedute:

Days Behind Schedute:

Problems / Delays

Safely Issues:

Accidents/Incidents:

Summary Of Work Performed Today

Signature:

Name:

Equipment On Site	No Units	Working	
		Yes	No

Employee /Contractor	Trade	Contracted Hours	Overtime

Materials Delivered	From & Rate	Equipment Rented	No Units

Notes:

Date:		**Day:**	Mon	Tue	Wed	Thu	Fri	Sat	Sun
Foreman:									
Contract No:									

Hours Lost Due To Bad Weather

Visitors

Weather Conditions

AM	PM

Schedule

Completion Date:	
Days Ahead of Schedute:	
Days Behind Schedute:	

Problems / Delays

Safely Issues:

Accidents/Incidents:

Summary Of Work Performed Today

Signature:	Name:

Equipment On Site	No Units	Working	
		Yes	No

Employee /Contractor	Trade	Contracted Hours	Overtime

Materials Delivered	From & Rate	Equipment Rented	No Units

Notes:

| Date: | | **Day:** | Mon | Tue | Wed | Thu | Fri | Sat | Sun |

Foreman:

Contract No:

Hours Lost Due To Bad Weather

Visitors

Weather Conditions

AM	PM

Schedule

Completion Date:

Days Ahead of Schedute:

Days Behind Schedute:

Problems / Delays

Safely Issues:

Accidents/Incidents:

Summary Of Work Performed Today

Signature:

Name:

Equipment On Site	No Units	Working	
		Yes	No

Employee /Contractor	Trade	Contracted Hours	Overtime

Materials Delivered	From & Rate	Equipment Rented	No Units

Notes:

Date:		**Day:**	Mon	Tue	Wed	Thu	Fri	Sat	Sun
Foreman:									
Contract No:									

Hours Lost Due To Bad Weather

Visitors

Weather Conditions

AM	PM

Schedule

Completion Date:

Days Ahead of Schedute:

Days Behind Schedute:

Problems / Delays

Safely Issues:

Accidents/Incidents:

Summary Of Work Performed Today

Signature:

Name:

Equipment On Site	No Units	Working	
		Yes	No

Employee /Contractor	Trade	Contracted Hours	Overtime

Materials Delivered	From & Rate	Equipment Rented	No Units

Notes:

Date:	**Day:**	Mon	Tue	Wed	Thu	Fri	Sat	Sun
Foreman:								
Contract No:								

Hours Lost Due To Bad Weather

Visitors

Weather Conditions

AM	PM

Schedule

Completion Date:

Days Ahead of Schedute:

Days Behind Schedute:

Problems / Delays

Safely Issues:

Accidents/Incidents:

Summary Of Work Performed Today

Signature:

Name:

Equipment On Site	No Units	Working	
		Yes	No

Employee /Contractor	Trade	Contracted Hours	Overtime

Materials Delivered	From & Rate	Equipment Rented	No Units

Notes:

Date:		**Day:**	Mon	Tue	Wed	Thu	Fri	Sat	Sun
Foreman:									
Contract No:									

Hours Lost Due To Bad Weather

Visitors

Weather Conditions

AM	PM

Schedule

Completion Date:	
Days Ahead of Schedute:	
Days Behind Schedule:	

Problems / Delays

Safely Issues:

Accidents/Incidents:

Summary Of Work Performed Today

Signature:	Name:

Equipment On Site	No Units	Working	
		Yes	No

Employee /Contractor	Trade	Contracted Hours	Overtime

Materials Delivered	From & Rate	Equipment Rented	No Units

Notes:

Date: **Day:** Mon Tue Wed Thu Fri Sat Sun

Foreman:

Contract No:

Hours Lost Due To Bad Weather

Visitors

Weather Conditions

AM	PM

Schedule

Completion Date:

Days Ahead of Schedute:

Days Behind Schedute:

Problems / Delays

Safely Issues:

Accidents/Incidents:

Summary Of Work Performed Today

Signature:

Name:

Equipment On Site	No Units	Working	
		Yes	No

Employee /Contractor	Trade	Contracted Hours	Overtime

Materials Delivered	From & Rate	Equipment Rented	No Units

Notes:

Date:		**Day:**	Mon	Tue	Wed	Thu	Fri	Sat	Sun
Foreman:									
Contract No:									

Hours Lost Due To Bad Weather

Visitors

Weather Conditions

AM	PM

Schedule

Completion Date:

Days Ahead of Schedute:

Days Behind Schedute:

Problems / Delays

Safely Issues:

Accidents/Incidents:

Summary Of Work Performed Today

Signature:

Name:

Equipment On Site	No Units	Working	
		Yes	No

Employee /Contractor	Trade	Contracted Hours	Overtime

Materials Delivered	From & Rate	Equipment Rented	No Units

Notes:

Date:		**Day:**	Mon	Tue	Wed	Thu	Fri	Sat	Sun

Foreman:

Contract No:

Hours Lost Due To Bad Weather

Visitors

Weather Conditions

AM	PM

Schedule

Completion Date:

Days Ahead of Schedute:

Days Behind Schedute:

Problems / Delays

Safely Issues:

Accidents/Incidents:

Summary Of Work Performed Today

Signature:

Name:

Equipment On Site	No Units	Working	
		Yes	No

Employee /Contractor	Trade	Contracted Hours	Overtime

Materials Delivered	From & Rate	Equipment Rented	No Units

Notes:

Date:		**Day:**	Mon	Tue	Wed	Thu	Fri	Sat	Sun

Foreman:

Contract No:

Hours Lost Due To Bad Weather

Visitors

Weather Conditions

AM	PM

Schedule

Completion Date:

Days Ahead of Schedute:

Days Behind Schedule:

Problems / Delays

Safely Issues:

Accidents/Incidents:

Summary Of Work Performed Today

Signature:	Name:

Equipment On Site	No Units	Working	
		Yes	No

Employee /Contractor	Trade	Contracted Hours	Overtime

Materials Delivered	From & Rate	Equipment Rented	No Units

Notes:

Date:		**Day:**	Mon	Tue	Wed	Thu	Fri	Sat	Sun
Foreman:									
Contract No:									

Hours Lost Due To Bad Weather

Visitors

Weather Conditions

AM	PM

Schedule

Completion Date:	
Days Ahead of Schedute:	
Days Behind Schedute:	

Problems / Delays

Safely Issues:

Accidents/Incidents:

Summary Of Work Performed Today

Signature:	Name:

Equipment On Site	No Units	Working	
		Yes	No

Employee /Contractor	Trade	Contracted Hours	Overtime

Materials Delivered	From & Rate	Equipment Rented	No Units

Notes:

<table>
<tr><td>Date:</td><td></td><td>Day:</td><td>Mon Tue Wed Thu Fri Sat Sun</td></tr>
<tr><td>Foreman:</td><td colspan="3"></td></tr>
<tr><td>Contract No:</td><td colspan="3"></td></tr>
</table>

Hours Lost Due To Bad Weather

Visitors

Weather Conditions

AM	PM

Schedule

Completion Date:

Days Ahead of Schedute:

Days Behind Schedute:

Problems / Delays

Safely Issues:

Accidents/Incidents:

Summary Of Work Performed Today

Signature:	Name:

Equipment On Site	No Units	Working	
		Yes	No

Employee /Contractor	Trade	Contracted Hours	Overtime

Materials Delivered	From & Rate	Equipment Rented	No Units

Notes:

Date:		**Day:**	Mon	Tue	Wed	Thu	Fri	Sat	Sun

Foreman:

Contract No:

Hours Lost Due To Bad Weather

Visitors

Weather Conditions

AM	PM

Schedule

Completion Date:

Days Ahead of Schedute:

Days Behind Schedute:

Problems / Delays

Safely Issues:

Accidents/Incidents:

Summary Of Work Performed Today

Signature:

Name:

Equipment On Site	No Units	Working	
		Yes	No

Employee /Contractor	Trade	Contracted Hours	Overtime

Materials Delivered	From & Rate	Equipment Rented	No Units

Notes:

Date:		**Day:**	Mon	Tue	Wed	Thu	Fri	Sat	Sun
Foreman:									
Contract No:									

Hours Lost Due To Bad Weather

Visitors

Weather Conditions

AM	PM

Schedule

Completion Date:

Days Ahead of Schedute:

Days Behind Schedute:

Problems / Delays

Safely Issues:

Accidents/Incidents:

Summary Of Work Performed Today

Signature:

Name:

Equipment On Site	No Units	Working	
		Yes	No

Employee /Contractor	Trade	Contracted Hours	Overtime

Materials Delivered	From & Rate	Equipment Rented	No Units

Notes:

Date:		**Day:**	Mon	Tue	Wed	Thu	Fri	Sat	Sun

Foreman:

Contract No:

Hours Lost Due To Bad Weather

Visitors

Weather Conditions

AM	PM

Schedule

Completion Date:

Days Ahead of Schedute:

Days Behind Schedute:

Problems / Delays

Safely Issues:

Accidents/Incidents:

Summary Of Work Performed Today

Signature:

Name:

Equipment On Site	No Units	Working	
		Yes	No

Employee /Contractor	Trade	Contracted Hours	Overtime

Materials Delivered	From & Rate	Equipment Rented	No Units

Notes:

Date:		**Day:**	Mon	Tue	Wed	Thu	Fri	Sat	Sun

Foreman:

Contract No:

Hours Lost Due To Bad Weather

Visitors

Weather Conditions

AM	PM

Schedule

Completion Date:

Days Ahead of Schedute:

Days Behind Schedute:

Problems / Delays

Safely Issues:

Accidents/Incidents:

Summary Of Work Performed Today

Signature:

Name:

Equipment On Site	No Units	Working	
		Yes	No

Employee /Contractor	Trade	Contracted Hours	Overtime

Materials Delivered	From & Rate	Equipment Rented	No Units

Notes:

Date:	Day:	Mon Tue Wed Thu Fri Sat Sun

Foreman:

Contract No:

Hours Lost Due To Bad Weather

Visitors

Weather Conditions

AM	PM

Schedule

Completion Date:

Days Ahead of Schedute:

Days Behind Schedute:

Problems / Delays

Safely Issues:

Accidents/Incidents:

Summary Of Work Performed Today

Signature:

Name:

Equipment On Site	No Units	Working	
		Yes	No

Employee /Contractor	Trade	Contracted Hours	Overtime

Materials Delivered	From & Rate	Equipment Rented	No Units

Notes:

Date:		Day:	Mon	Tue	Wed	Thu	Fri	Sat	Sun

Foreman:

Contract No:

Hours Lost Due To Bad Weather

Visitors

Weather Conditions

AM	PM

Schedule

Completion Date:

Days Ahead of Schedute:

Days Behind Schedute:

Problems / Delays

Safely Issues:

Accidents/Incidents:

Summary Of Work Performed Today

Signature:

Name:

Equipment On Site	No Units	Working	
		Yes	No

Employee /Contractor	Trade	Contracted Hours	Overtime

Materials Delivered	From & Rate	Equipment Rented	No Units

Notes:

Date:		**Day:**	Mon	Tue	Wed	Thu	Fri	Sat	Sun

Foreman:

Contract No:

Hours Lost Due To Bad Weather

Visitors

Weather Conditions

AM	PM

Schedule

Completion Date:

Days Ahead of Schedute:

Days Behind Schedute:

Problems / Delays

Safely Issues:

Accidents/Incidents:

Summary Of Work Performed Today

Signature:

Name:

Equipment On Site	No Units	Working	
		Yes	No

Employee /Contractor	Trade	Contracted Hours	Overtime

Materials Delivered	From & Rate	Equipment Rented	No Units

Notes:

Date:		**Day:**	Mon	Tue	Wed	Thu	Fri	Sat	Sun

Foreman:

Contract No:

Hours Lost Due To Bad Weather

Visitors

Weather Conditions

AM	PM

Schedule

Completion Date:

Days Ahead of Schedute:

Days Behind Schedute:

Problems / Delays

Safely Issues:

Accidents/Incidents:

Summary Of Work Performed Today

Signature:

Name:

Equipment On Site	No Units	Working	
		Yes	No

Employee /Contractor	Trade	Contracted Hours	Overtime

Materials Delivered	From & Rate	Equipment Rented	No Units

Notes:

Date:		Day:	Mon	Tue	Wed	Thu	Fri	Sat	Sun
Foreman:									
Contract No:									

Hours Lost Due To Bad Weather

Visitors

Weather Conditions

AM	PM

Schedule

Completion Date:	
Days Ahead of Schedute:	
Days Behind Schedute:	

Problems / Delays

Safely Issues:

Accidents/Incidents:

Summary Of Work Performed Today

Signature:	Name:

Equipment On Site	No Units	Working	
		Yes	No

Employee /Contractor	Trade	Contracted Hours	Overtime

Materials Delivered	From & Rate	Equipment Rented	No Units

Notes:

Date:		**Day:**	Mon	Tue	Wed	Thu	Fri	Sat	Sun

Foreman:

Contract No:

Hours Lost Due To Bad Weather

Visitors

Weather Conditions

AM	PM

Schedule

Completion Date:	
Days Ahead of Schedute:	
Days Behind Schedute:	

Problems / Delays

Safely Issues:

Accidents/Incidents:

Summary Of Work Performed Today

Signature:

Name:

Equipment On Site	No Units	Working	
		Yes	No

Employee /Contractor	Trade	Contracted Hours	Overtime

Materials Delivered	From & Rate	Equipment Rented	No Units

Notes:

Date:		**Day:**	Mon	Tue	Wed	Thu	Fri	Sat	Sun
Foreman:									
Contract No:									

Hours Lost Due To Bad Weather

Visitors

Weather Conditions

AM	PM

Schedule

Completion Date:

Days Ahead of Schedute:

Days Behind Schedute:

Problems / Delays

Safely Issues:

Accidents/Incidents:

Summary Of Work Performed Today

Signature:

Name:

Equipment On Site	No Units	Working	
		Yes	No

Employee /Contractor	Trade	Contracted Hours	Overtime

Materials Delivered	From & Rate	Equipment Rented	No Units

Notes:

Date:		**Day:**	Mon	Tue	Wed	Thu	Fri	Sat	Sun

Foreman:

Contract No:

Hours Lost Due To Bad Weather

Visitors

Weather Conditions

AM	PM

Schedule

Completion Date:
Days Ahead of Schedute:
Days Behind Schedute:

Problems / Delays

Safely Issues:

Accidents/Incidents:

Summary Of Work Performed Today

Signature:	Name:

Equipment On Site	No Units	Working	
		Yes	No

Employee /Contractor	Trade	Contracted Hours	Overtime

Materials Delivered	From & Rate	Equipment Rented	No Units

Notes:

Date:	**Day:**	Mon	Tue	Wed	Thu	Fri	Sat	Sun

Foreman:

Contract No:

Hours Lost Due To Bad Weather	Visitors

Weather Conditions	
AM	PM

Schedule

Completion Date:

Days Ahead of Schedute:

Days Behind Schedute:

Problems / Delays

Safely Issues:

Accidents/Incidents:

Summary Of Work Performed Today

Signature:

Name:

Equipment On Site	No Units	Working	
		Yes	No

Employee /Contractor	Trade	Contracted Hours	Overtime

Materials Delivered	From & Rate	Equipment Rented	No Units

Notes:

Date:		**Day:**	Mon	Tue	Wed	Thu	Fri	Sat	Sun
Foreman:									
Contract No:									

Hours Lost Due To Bad Weather

Visitors

Weather Conditions

AM	PM

Schedule

Completion Date:

Days Ahead of Schedute:

Days Behind Schedute:

Problems / Delays

Safely Issues:

Accidents/Incidents:

Summary Of Work Performed Today

Signature:

Name:

Equipment On Site	No Units	Working	
		Yes	No

Employee /Contractor	Trade	Contracted Hours	Overtime

Materials Delivered	From & Rate	Equipment Rented	No Units

Notes:

Date:		**Day:**	Mon	Tue	Wed	Thu	Fri	Sat	Sun
Foreman:									
Contract No:									

Hours Lost Due To Bad Weather

Visitors

Weather Conditions

AM	PM

Schedule

Completion Date:

Days Ahead of Schedute:

Days Behind Schedute:

Problems / Delays

Safely Issues:

Accidents/Incidents:

Summary Of Work Performed Today

Signature:

Name:

Equipment On Site	No Units	Working	
		Yes	No

Employee /Contractor	Trade	Contracted Hours	Overtime

Materials Delivered	From & Rate	Equipment Rented	No Units

Notes:

| Date: | | **Day:** | Mon | Tue | Wed | Thu | Fri | Sat | Sun |

Foreman:

Contract No:

Hours Lost Due To Bad Weather

Visitors

Weather Conditions

AM	PM

Schedule

Completion Date:

Days Ahead of Schedute:

Days Behind Schedute:

Problems / Delays

Safely Issues:

Accidents/Incidents:

Summary Of Work Performed Today

Signature:

Name:

Equipment On Site	No Units	Working	
		Yes	No

Employee /Contractor	Trade	Contracted Hours	Overtime

Materials Delivered	From & Rate	Equipment Rented	No Units

Notes:

Date:		**Day:**	Mon	Tue	Wed	Thu	Fri	Sat	Sun
Foreman:									
Contract No:									

Hours Lost Due To Bad Weather

Visitors

Weather Conditions

AM	PM

Schedule

Completion Date:	
Days Ahead of Schedute:	
Days Behind Schedute:	

Problems / Delays

Safely Issues:

Accidents/Incidents:

Summary Of Work Performed Today

Signature:	Name:

Equipment On Site	No Units	Working	
		Yes	No

Employee /Contractor	Trade	Contracted Hours	Overtime

Materials Delivered	From & Rate	Equipment Rented	No Units

Notes:

| Date: | | **Day:** | Mon | Tue | Wed | Thu | Fri | Sat | Sun |

Foreman:

Contract No:

Hours Lost Due To Bad Weather

Visitors

Weather Conditions

AM	PM

Schedule

Completion Date:

Days Ahead of Schedute:

Days Behind Schedute:

Problems / Delays

Safely Issues:

Accidents/Incidents:

Summary Of Work Performed Today

Signature:

Name:

Equipment On Site	No Units	Working	
		Yes	No

Employee /Contractor	Trade	Contracted Hours	Overtime

Materials Delivered	From & Rate	Equipment Rented	No Units

Notes:

| Date: | | **Day:** | Mon | Tue | Wed | Thu | Fri | Sat | Sun |

| Foreman: |
| Contract No: |

Hours Lost Due To Bad Weather

Visitors

Weather Conditions

| AM | PM |

Schedule

Completion Date:

Days Ahead of Schedute:

Days Behind Schedute:

Problems / Delays

Safely Issues:

Accidents/Incidents:

Summary Of Work Performed Today

| Signature: | Name: |

Equipment On Site	No Units	Working	
		Yes	No

Employee /Contractor	Trade	Contracted Hours	Overtime

Materials Delivered	From & Rate	Equipment Rented	No Units

Notes:

Date:		**Day:**	Mon	Tue	Wed	Thu	Fri	Sat	Sun
Foreman:									
Contract No:									

Hours Lost Due To Bad Weather	Visitors

Weather Conditions	
AM	PM

Schedule		Problems / Delays
Completion Date:		
Days Ahead of Schedute:		
Days Behind Schedute:		

Safely Issues:	Accidents/Incidents:

Summary Of Work Performed Today

Signature:	Name:

Equipment On Site	No Units	Working	
		Yes	No

Employee /Contractor	Trade	Contracted Hours	Overtime

Materials Delivered	From & Rate	Equipment Rented	No Units

Notes:

<table>
<tr><td>Date:</td><td></td><td>Day: Mon Tue Wed Thu Fri Sat Sun</td></tr>
<tr><td>Foreman:</td><td colspan="2"></td></tr>
<tr><td>Contract No:</td><td colspan="2"></td></tr>
</table>

Hours Lost Due To Bad Weather

Visitors

Weather Conditions

AM	PM

Schedule

Completion Date:	
Days Ahead of Schedute:	
Days Behind Schedute:	

Problems / Delays

Safely Issues:

Accidents/Incidents:

Summary Of Work Performed Today

Signature:	Name:

Equipment On Site	No Units	Working	
		Yes	No

Employee /Contractor	Trade	Contracted Hours	Overtime

Materials Delivered	From & Rate	Equipment Rented	No Units

Notes:

Date:		**Day:**	Mon	Tue	Wed	Thu	Fri	Sat	Sun

Foreman:

Contract No:

Hours Lost Due To Bad Weather

Visitors

Weather Conditions

AM	PM

Schedule

Completion Date:
Days Ahead of Schedute:
Days Behind Schedute:

Problems / Delays

Safely Issues:

Accidents/Incidents:

Summary Of Work Performed Today

Signature:	Name:

Equipment On Site	No Units	Working	
		Yes	No

Employee /Contractor	Trade	Contracted Hours	Overtime

Materials Delivered	From & Rate	Equipment Rented	No Units

Notes:

Date:		**Day:**	Mon	Tue	Wed	Thu	Fri	Sat	Sun
Foreman:									
Contract No:									

Hours Lost Due To Bad Weather

Visitors

Weather Conditions

AM	PM

Schedule

Completion Date:	
Days Ahead of Schedute:	
Days Behind Schedute:	

Problems / Delays

Safely Issues:

Accidents/Incidents:

Summary Of Work Performed Today

Signature:	Name:

Equipment On Site	No Units	Working	
		Yes	No

Employee /Contractor	Trade	Contracted Hours	Overtime

Materials Delivered	From & Rate	Equipment Rented	No Units

Notes:

Date:		**Day:**	Mon	Tue	Wed	Thu	Fri	Sat	Sun

Foreman:

Contract No:

Hours Lost Due To Bad Weather

Visitors

Weather Conditions

AM	PM

Schedule

Completion Date:

Days Ahead of Schedute:

Days Behind Schedute:

Problems / Delays

Safely Issues:

Accidents/Incidents:

Summary Of Work Performed Today

Signature:

Name:

Equipment On Site	No Units	Working	
		Yes	No

Employee /Contractor	Trade	Contracted Hours	Overtime

Materials Delivered	From & Rate	Equipment Rented	No Units

Notes:

| Date: | | **Day:** | Mon | Tue | Wed | Thu | Fri | Sat | Sun |

Foreman:

Contract No:

Hours Lost Due To Bad Weather

Visitors

Weather Conditions

AM	PM

Schedule

Completion Date:

Days Ahead of Schedute:

Days Behind Schedute:

Problems / Delays

Safely Issues:

Accidents/Incidents:

Summary Of Work Performed Today

Signature:

Name:

Equipment On Site	No Units	Working	
		Yes	No

Employee /Contractor	Trade	Contracted Hours	Overtime

Materials Delivered	From & Rate	Equipment Rented	No Units

Notes:

Date:		**Day:**	Mon	Tue	Wed	Thu	Fri	Sat	Sun

Foreman:

Contract No:

Hours Lost Due To Bad Weather	Visitors

Weather Conditions

AM	PM

Schedule

Completion Date:	
Days Ahead of Schedute:	
Days Behind Schedute:	

Problems / Delays

Safely Issues:

Accidents/Incidents:

Summary Of Work Performed Today

Signature:	Name:

Equipment On Site	No Units	Working	
		Yes	No

Employee /Contractor	Trade	Contracted Hours	Overtime

Materials Delivered	From & Rate	Equipment Rented	No Units

Notes:

Date:		**Day:**	Mon	Tue	Wed	Thu	Fri	Sat	Sun

Foreman:

Contract No:

Hours Lost Due To Bad Weather | Visitors

Weather Conditions

AM	PM

Schedule | Problems / Delays

Completion Date:

Days Ahead of Schedute:

Days Behind Schedute:

Safely Issues: | Accidents/Incidents:

Summary Of Work Performed Today

Signature:

Name:

Equipment On Site	No Units	Working	
		Yes	No

Employee /Contractor	Trade	Contracted Hours	Overtime

Materials Delivered	From & Rate	Equipment Rented	No Units

Notes:

Date:		**Day:**	Mon	Tue	Wed	Thu	Fri	Sat	Sun

Foreman:

Contract No:

Hours Lost Due To Bad Weather

Visitors

Weather Conditions

AM	PM

Schedule

Completion Date:

Days Ahead of Schedute:

Days Behind Schedute:

Problems / Delays

Safely Issues:

Accidents/Incidents:

Summary Of Work Performed Today

Signature:

Name:

Equipment On Site	No Units	Working	
		Yes	No

Employee /Contractor	Trade	Contracted Hours	Overtime

Materials Delivered	From & Rate	Equipment Rented	No Units

Notes:

| Date: | | **Day:** | Mon | Tue | Wed | Thu | Fri | Sat | Sun |

| Foreman: |
| Contract No: |

Hours Lost Due To Bad Weather

Visitors

Weather Conditions

AM	PM

Schedule

Completion Date:

Days Ahead of Schedute:

Days Behind Schedute:

Problems / Delays

Safely Issues:

Accidents/Incidents:

Summary Of Work Performed Today

| Signature: | Name: |

Equipment On Site	No Units	Working	
		Yes	No

Employee /Contractor	Trade	Contracted Hours	Overtime

Materials Delivered	From & Rate	Equipment Rented	No Units

Notes:

Date:		Day:	Mon	Tue	Wed	Thu	Fri	Sat	Sun
Foreman:									
Contract No:									

Hours Lost Due To Bad Weather

Visitors

Weather Conditions

AM	PM

Schedule

Completion Date:

Days Ahead of Schedute:

Days Behind Schedute:

Problems / Delays

Safely Issues:

Accidents/Incidents:

Summary Of Work Performed Today

Signature:

Name:

Equipment On Site	No Units	Working	
		Yes	No

Employee /Contractor	Trade	Contracted Hours	Overtime

Materials Delivered	From & Rate	Equipment Rented	No Units

Notes:

Date:		**Day:**	Mon	Tue	Wed	Thu	Fri	Sat	Sun

Foreman:

Contract No:

Hours Lost Due To Bad Weather

Visitors

Weather Conditions

AM	PM

Schedule

Completion Date:

Days Ahead of Schedute:

Days Behind Schedute:

Problems / Delays

Safely Issues:

Accidents/Incidents:

Summary Of Work Performed Today

Signature:

Name:

Equipment On Site	No Units	Working	
		Yes	No

Employee /Contractor	Trade	Contracted Hours	Overtime

Materials Delivered	From & Rate	Equipment Rented	No Units

Notes:

Date:		**Day:**	Mon	Tue	Wed	Thu	Fri	Sat	Sun
Foreman:									
Contract No:									

Hours Lost Due To Bad Weather	Visitors

Weather Conditions

AM	PM

Schedule	Problems / Delays
Completion Date:	
Days Ahead of Schedute:	
Days Behind Schedute:	

Safely Issues:	Accidents/Incidents:

Summary Of Work Performed Today

Signature:	Name:

Equipment On Site	No Units	Working	
		Yes	No

Employee /Contractor	Trade	Contracted Hours	Overtime

Materials Delivered	From & Rate	Equipment Rented	No Units

Notes:

| Date: | | **Day:** | Mon | Tue | Wed | Thu | Fri | Sat | Sun |

| Foreman: | |

| Contract No: | |

Hours Lost Due To Bad Weather

Visitors

Weather Conditions

AM	PM

Schedule

Completion Date:	
Days Ahead of Schedute:	
Days Behind Schedule:	

Problems / Delays

Safely Issues:

Accidents/Incidents:

Summary Of Work Performed Today

| Signature: | Name: |

Equipment On Site	No Units	Working	
		Yes	No

Employee /Contractor	Trade	Contracted Hours	Overtime

Materials Delivered	From & Rate	Equipment Rented	No Units

Notes:

Date:		**Day:**	Mon	Tue	Wed	Thu	Fri	Sat	Sun

Foreman:

Contract No:

Hours Lost Due To Bad Weather

Visitors

Weather Conditions

AM	PM

Schedule

Completion Date:

Days Ahead of Schedute:

Days Behind Schedute:

Problems / Delays

Safely Issues:

Accidents/Incidents:

Summary Of Work Performed Today

Signature:	Name:

Equipment On Site	No Units	Working	
		Yes	No

Employee /Contractor	Trade	Contracted Hours	Overtime

Materials Delivered	From & Rate	Equipment Rented	No Units

Notes:

Date:		**Day:**	Mon	Tue	Wed	Thu	Fri	Sat	Sun
Foreman:									
Contract No:									

Hours Lost Due To Bad Weather	Visitors

Weather Conditions

AM	PM

Schedule	Problems / Delays
Completion Date:	
Days Ahead of Schedute:	
Days Behind Schedute:	

Safely Issues:	Accidents/Incidents:

Summary Of Work Performed Today

Signature:	Name:

Equipment On Site	No Units	Working	
		Yes	No

Employee /Contractor	Trade	Contracted Hours	Overtime

Materials Delivered	From & Rate	Equipment Rented	No Units

Notes:

Date:		**Day:**	Mon	Tue	Wed	Thu	Fri	Sat	Sun

Foreman:

Contract No:

Hours Lost Due To Bad Weather

Visitors

Weather Conditions

AM	PM

Schedule

Completion Date:

Days Ahead of Schedute:

Days Behind Schedute:

Problems / Delays

Safely Issues:

Accidents/Incidents:

Summary Of Work Performed Today

Signature:	Name:

Equipment On Site	No Units	Working	
		Yes	No

Employee /Contractor	Trade	Contracted Hours	Overtime

Materials Delivered	From & Rate	Equipment Rented	No Units

Notes:

| Date: | | **Day:** | Mon | Tue | Wed | Thu | Fri | Sat | Sun |

Foreman:

Contract No:

Hours Lost Due To Bad Weather

Visitors

Weather Conditions

AM	PM

Schedule

Completion Date:

Days Ahead of Schedute:

Days Behind Schedute:

Problems / Delays

Safely Issues:

Accidents/Incidents:

Summary Of Work Performed Today

Signature:

Name:

Equipment On Site	No Units	Working	
		Yes	No

Employee /Contractor	Trade	Contracted Hours	Overtime

Materials Delivered	From & Rate	Equipment Rented	No Units

Notes:

Date:		**Day:**	Mon	Tue	Wed	Thu	Fri	Sat	Sun
Foreman:									
Contract No:									

Hours Lost Due To Bad Weather

Visitors

Weather Conditions

AM	PM

Schedule

Completion Date:

Days Ahead of Schedute:

Days Behind Schedute:

Problems / Delays

Safely Issues:

Accidents/Incidents:

Summary Of Work Performed Today

Signature:

Name:

Equipment On Site	No Units	Working	
		Yes	No

Employee /Contractor	Trade	Contracted Hours	Overtime

Materials Delivered	From & Rate	Equipment Rented	No Units

Notes:

Date:		**Day:**	Mon	Tue	Wed	Thu	Fri	Sat	Sun
Foreman:									
Contract No:									

Hours Lost Due To Bad Weather

Visitors

Weather Conditions

AM	PM

Schedule

Completion Date:

Days Ahead of Schedute:

Days Behind Schedute:

Problems / Delays

Safely Issues:

Accidents/Incidents:

Summary Of Work Performed Today

Signature:	Name:

Equipment On Site	No Units	Working	
		Yes	No

Employee /Contractor	Trade	Contracted Hours	Overtime

Materials Delivered	From & Rate	Equipment Rented	No Units

Notes:

Date:		**Day:**	Mon	Tue	Wed	Thu	Fri	Sat	Sun

Foreman:

Contract No:

Hours Lost Due To Bad Weather

Visitors

Weather Conditions

AM	PM

Schedule

Completion Date:

Days Ahead of Schedute:

Days Behind Schedule:

Problems / Delays

Safely Issues:

Accidents/Incidents:

Summary Of Work Performed Today

Signature:

Name:

Equipment On Site	No Units	Working	
		Yes	No

Employee /Contractor	Trade	Contracted Hours	Overtime

Materials Delivered	From & Rate	Equipment Rented	No Units

Notes:

Date:		**Day:**	Mon	Tue	Wed	Thu	Fri	Sat	Sun
Foreman:									
Contract No:									

Hours Lost Due To Bad Weather	Visitors

Weather Conditions

AM	PM

Schedule	Problems / Delays
Completion Date:	
Days Ahead of Schedute:	
Days Behind Schedute:	

Safely Issues:	Accidents/Incidents:

Summary Of Work Performed Today

Signature:	Name:

Equipment On Site	No Units	Working	
		Yes	No

Employee /Contractor	Trade	Contracted Hours	Overtime

Materials Delivered	From & Rate	Equipment Rented	No Units

Notes:

Date:		**Day:**	Mon	Tue	Wed	Thu	Fri	Sat	Sun
Foreman:									
Contract No:									

Hours Lost Due To Bad Weather

Visitors

Weather Conditions

AM	PM

Schedule

Completion Date:

Days Ahead of Schedute:

Days Behind Schedute:

Problems / Delays

Safely Issues:

Accidents/Incidents:

Summary Of Work Performed Today

Signature:

Name:

Equipment On Site	No Units	Working	
		Yes	No

Employee /Contractor	Trade	Contracted Hours	Overtime

Materials Delivered	From & Rate	Equipment Rented	No Units

Notes:

| Date: | | **Day:** | Mon | Tue | Wed | Thu | Fri | Sat | Sun |

Foreman:

Contract No:

Hours Lost Due To Bad Weather

Visitors

Weather Conditions

AM	PM

Schedule

Completion Date:

Days Ahead of Schedute:

Days Behind Schedule:

Problems / Delays

Safely Issues:

Accidents/Incidents:

Summary Of Work Performed Today

Signature:

Name:

Equipment On Site	No Units	Working	
		Yes	No

Employee /Contractor	Trade	Contracted Hours	Overtime

Materials Delivered	From & Rate	Equipment Rented	No Units

Notes:

Date:	**Day:**	Mon	Tue	Wed	Thu	Fri	Sat	Sun
Foreman:								
Contract No:								

Hours Lost Due To Bad Weather

Visitors

Weather Conditions

AM	PM

Schedule

Completion Date:

Days Ahead of Schedute:

Days Behind Schedute:

Problems / Delays

Safely Issues:

Accidents/Incidents:

Summary Of Work Performed Today

Signature:

Name:

Equipment On Site	No Units	Working	
		Yes	No

Employee /Contractor	Trade	Contracted Hours	Overtime

Materials Delivered	From & Rate	Equipment Rented	No Units

Notes: